Savior
Born on Christmas Morn

The Story of Jesus' Birth, Luke 2:1–20 for children
Melinda Kay Busch • Illustrated by Melanie Hall

Text © 2003 Concordia Publishing House, 3558 S. Jefferson Avenue, St. Louis, MO 63118-3968
1-800-325-3040 • www.cph.org

Illustrations © 2003 Melanie Hall, Olivebridge, NY

All rights reserved. No part of this publication may be reproduced, stored in a retrieval system, or transmitted, in any form or by any means, electronic, mechanical, photocopying, recording, or otherwise, without the prior written permission of Concordia Publishing House.

Manufactured in United States of America.

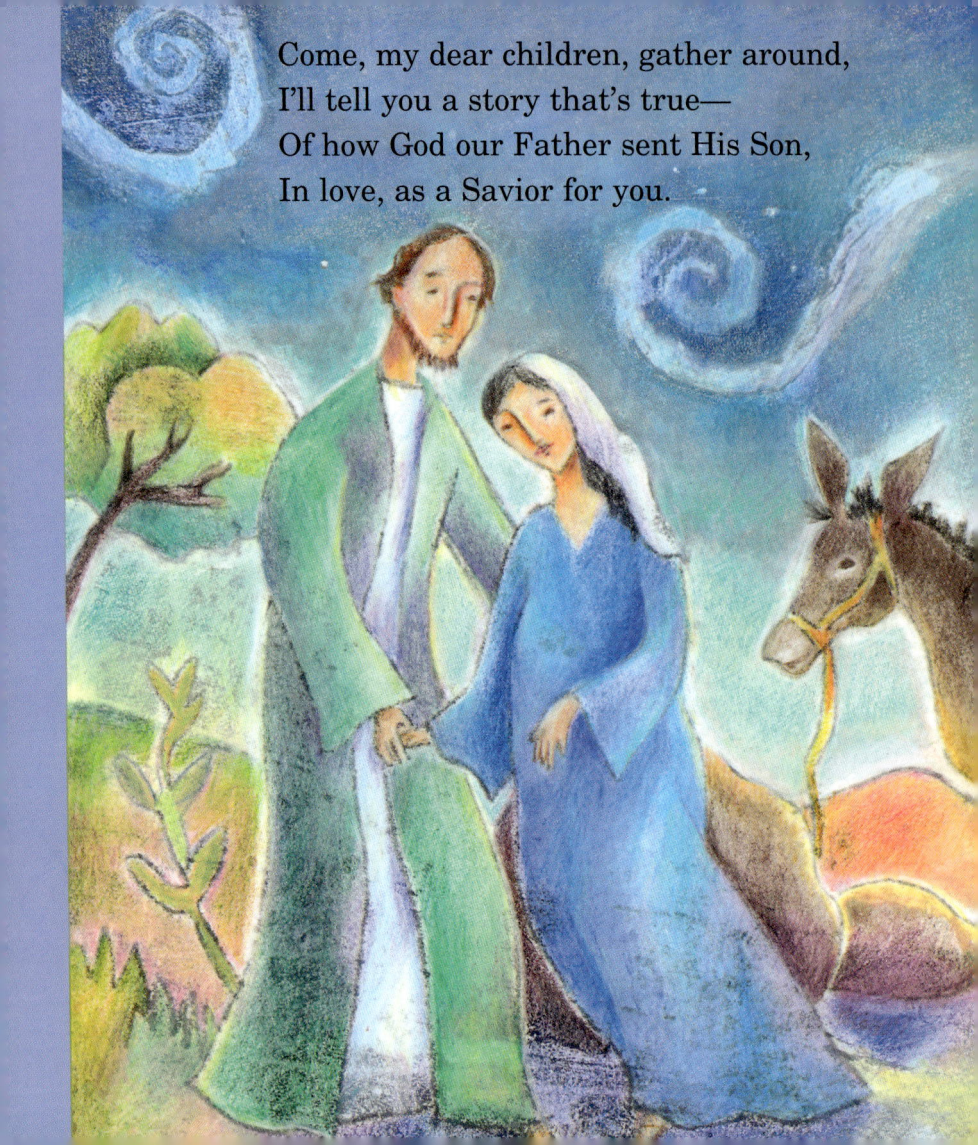

Come, my dear children, gather around,
I'll tell you a story that's true—
Of how God our Father sent His Son,
In love, as a Savior for you.

Mary and Joseph traveled for days,
Obeying great Caesar's decree
To go to their ancestral city,
To be counted and taxed properly.

Joseph was born of King David's line,
To Bethlehem he had to go,
For this was the City of David,
Who had lived many years ago.

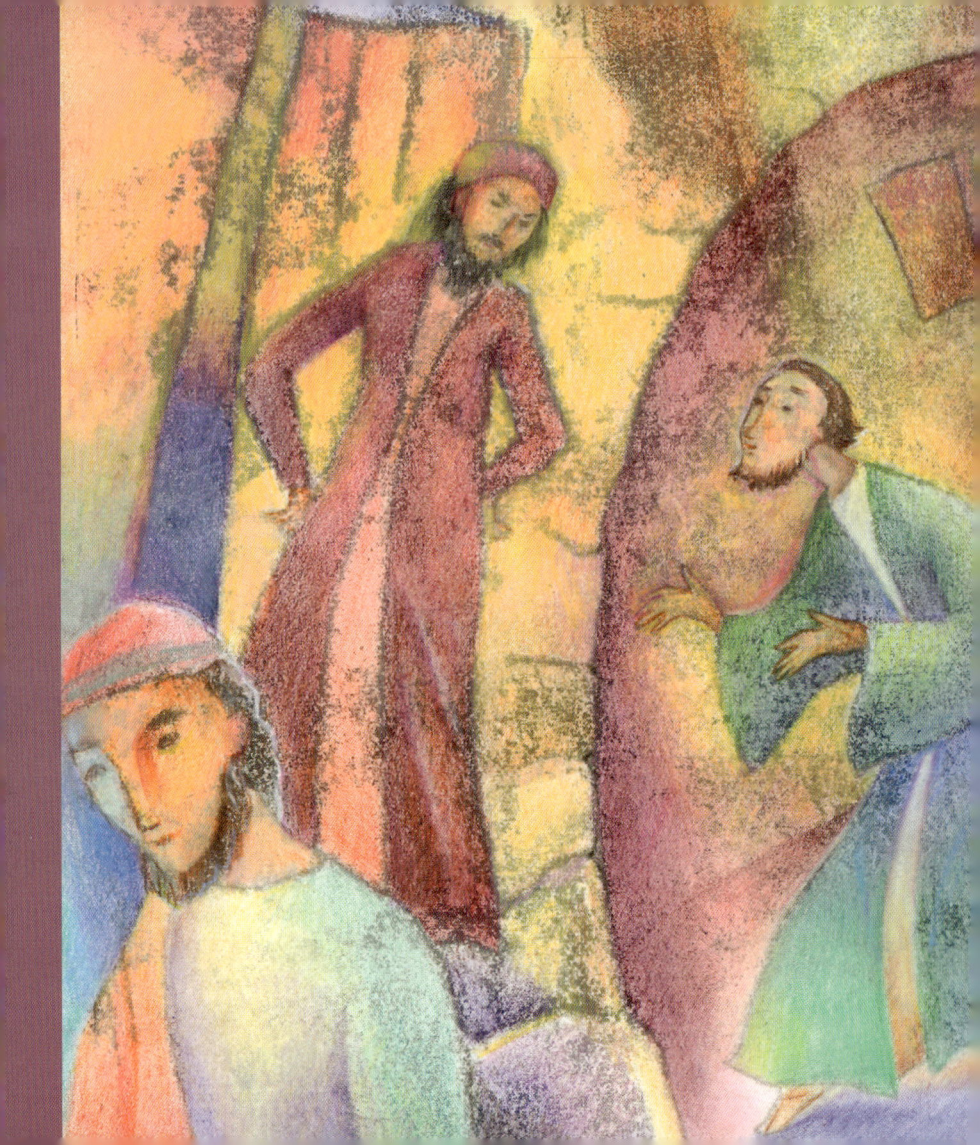

So even though Mary was weary,
Expecting her child any day,
They packed up their bags and they started
On a long and difficult way.

But when they arrived feeling tired,
All weary and longing for rest,
They found all the inns were too crowded
To make room for another guest.

A kind innkeeper pitied their plight
And guided them to his stable.
"You can sleep here tonight if you wish.
I'll bring fresh hay when I'm able."

There in the stable Mary gave birth,
And cradled sweet Jesus so warm.
And though He was tiny and helpless,
He was God in infant form.

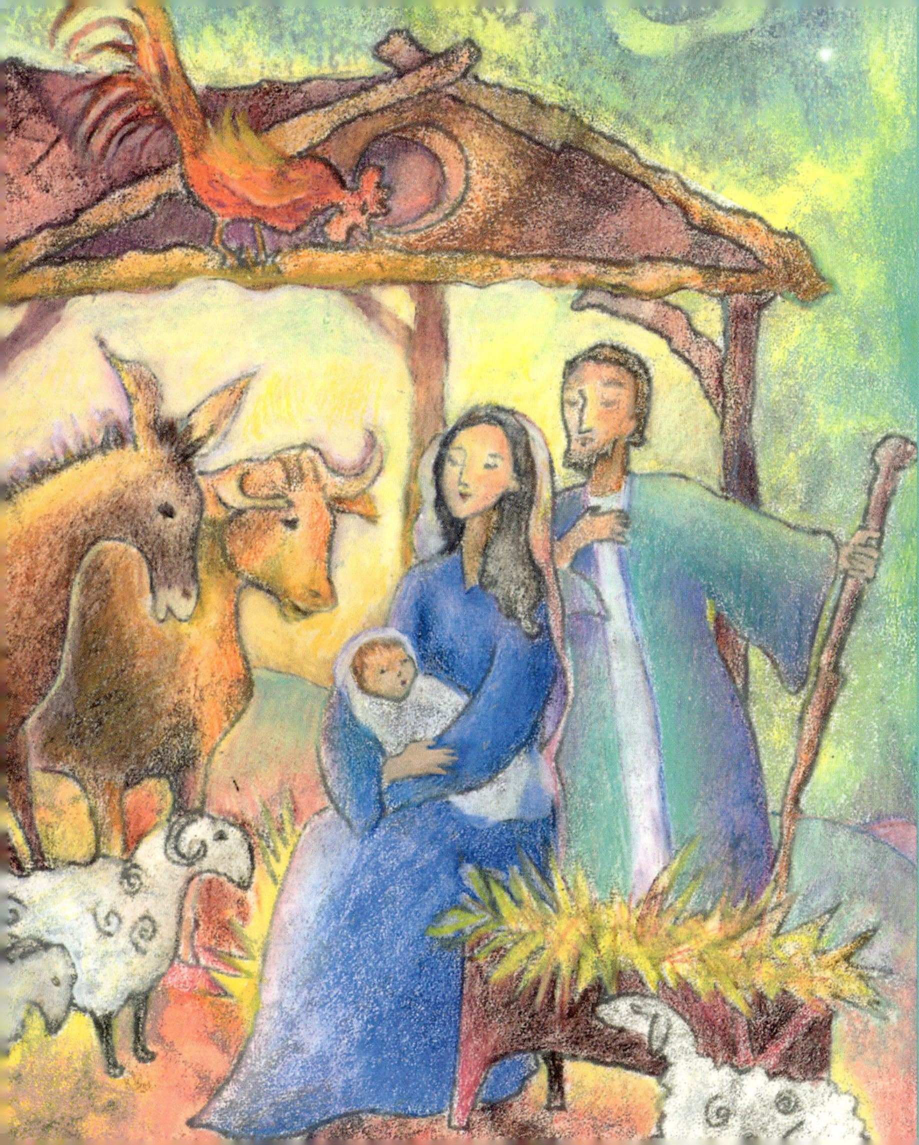

Just outside Bethlehem, not far away,
Shepherds guarded their sheep in the night.
Suddenly the sky lit up like day,
And the glory of God shone bright.

Amazed, the shepherds fell to their knees.
They shivered and cowered in fear,
For an angel of God appeared to them
And spoke in a voice loud and clear.

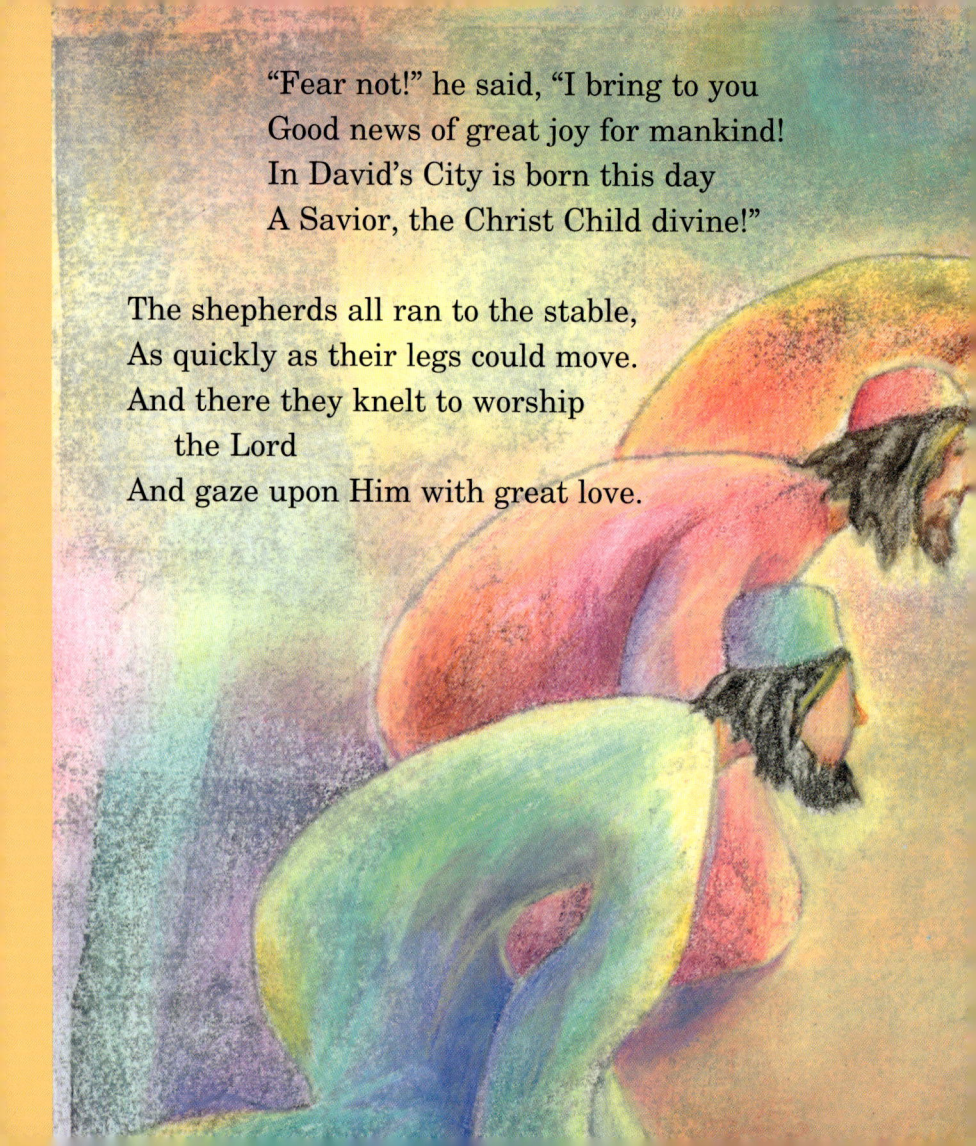

"Fear not!" he said, "I bring to you
Good news of great joy for mankind!
In David's City is born this day
A Savior, the Christ Child divine!"

The shepherds all ran to the stable,
As quickly as their legs could move.
And there they knelt to worship
   the Lord
And gaze upon Him with great love.

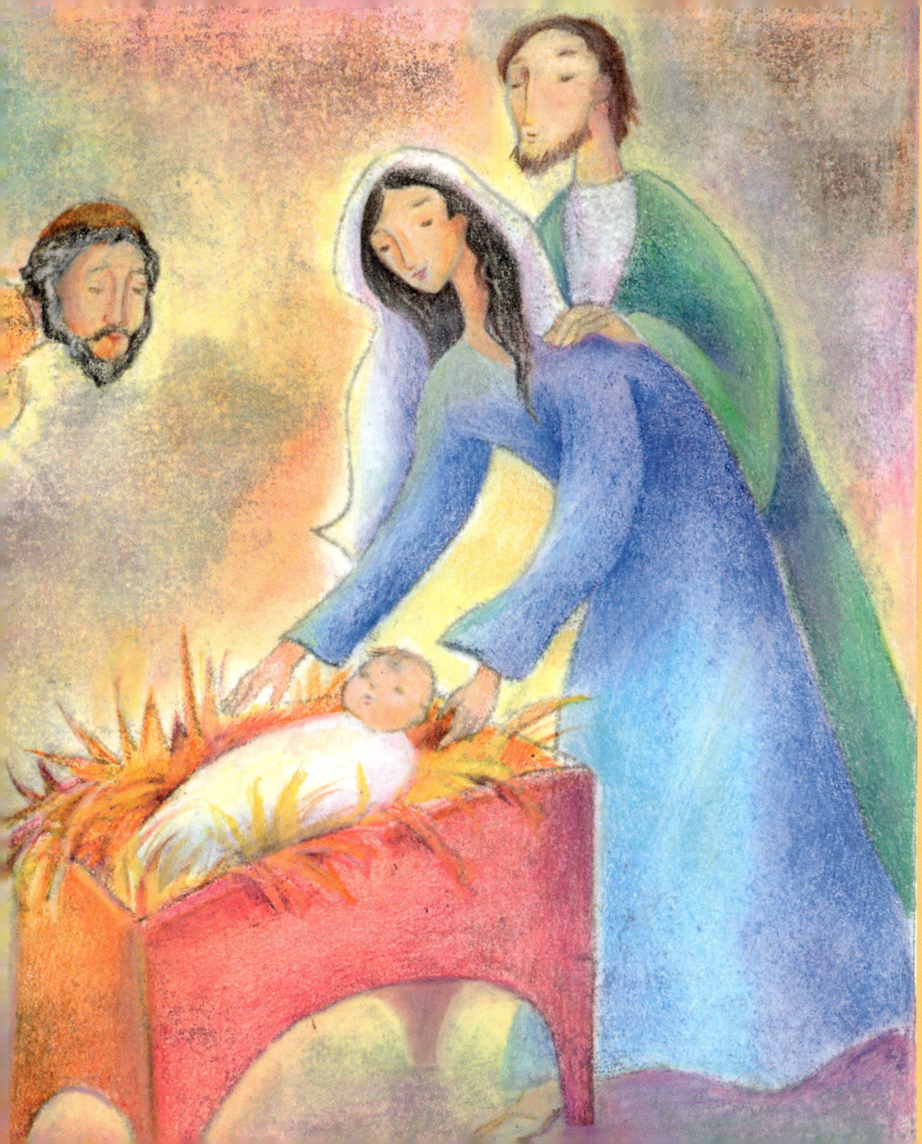

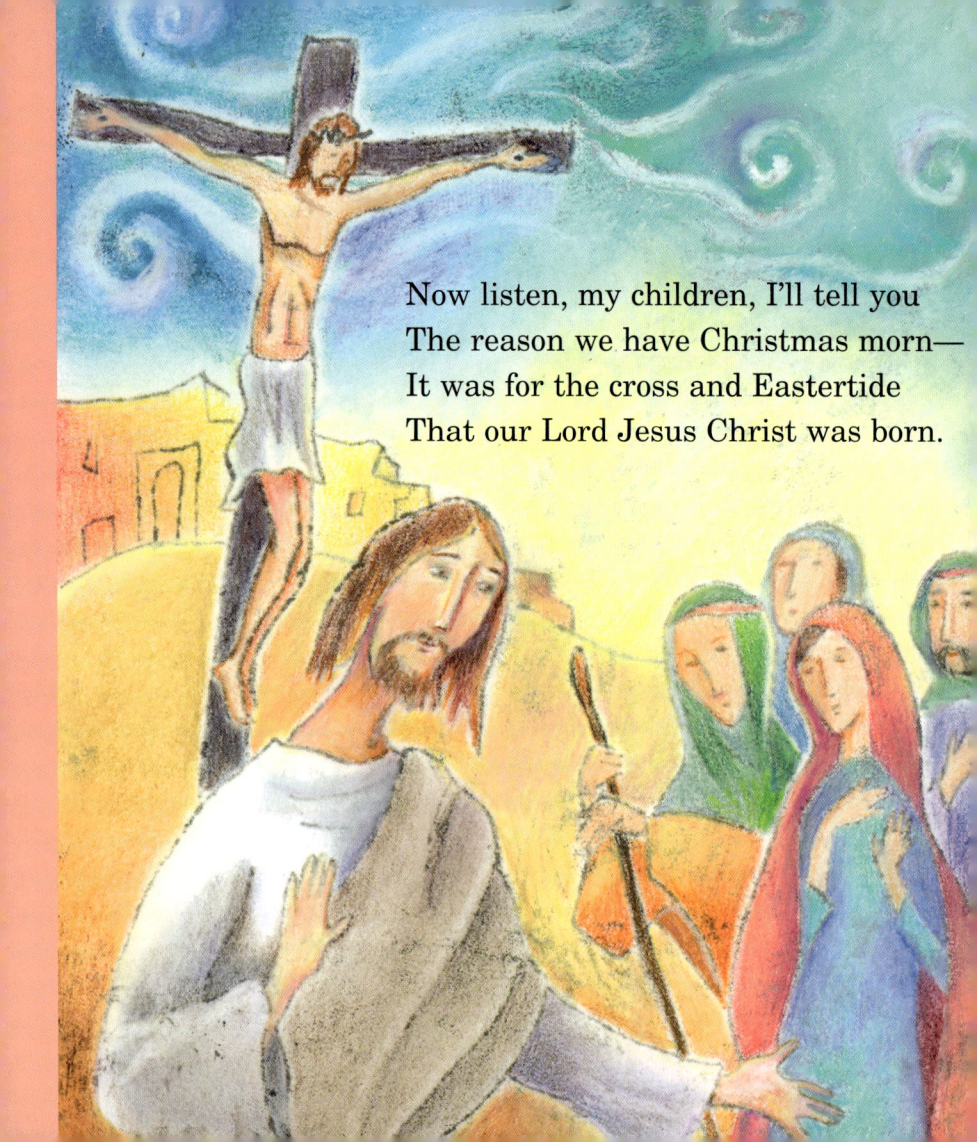

Now listen, my children, I'll tell you
The reason we have Christmas morn—
It was for the cross and Eastertide
That our Lord Jesus Christ was born.

He came here to love and to teach us.
He came here to heal and to pray.
But most of all the Messiah came
To die on a cross one sad day.

For we all have hearts that are sinful—
We have broken God's heart in two.
And only the death of our Savior
Can give us a life that is new.

But do not forget the story's end—
Christ did not remain in the grave!
He rose again on Easter morn
And He lives to love and to save!

So come now, my children, be joyful.
Celebrate this day with great cheer,
For Jesus was born on Christmas morn,
As a gift for all, far and near!

Dear Parents,

The great hymn, *Savior of the Nations, Come* unpacks the miracle of the two natures of Christ (human and divine). The simple truth that God is man is both a profound mystery and a simple confession.

As the hymn focuses upon the two natures of Christ it also rejoices that the God man has come to be the Savior of the Nations. The promise made to Abraham (Genesis 12) now finds fulfillment in the child of the promise. He comes to rescue and redeem all that once was His. Certainly there would be no nations of the world had not sin, death, and the power of the devil overtaken us in the garden. The consequences of sin find brother fighting against brother and nation against nation.

Yet despite our sinful divisions, the Christ comes to make us whole. He comes for all the Nations of the World to reveal Himself as the long-expected Jesus.

He comes for YOU!

The Editor